Our World — of — Wonders

Written by Yanitzia Canetti

STECK-VAUGHN
ELEMENTARY · SECONDARY · ADULT · LIBRARY

A Harcourt Classroom Education Company

www.steck-vaughn.com

CONTENTS

INTRODUCTION

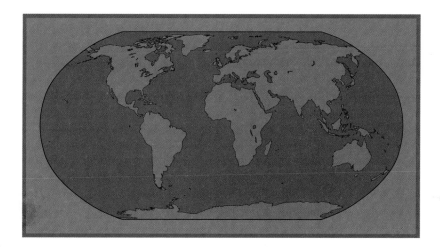

"I'm off to see the world!" We hear people say this in movies and cartoons. We read it in books. You may have even said it yourself. What does it mean to see the world?

We see the world when we look at a globe. We see it when we look at maps. But "to see the world" means something else, too. To see the world is to travel to new places and learn about them. You do these things when you study **geography**. Our world is full of wonderful places, and this book can take you to them. Let's go!

CHAPTER ONE

France's Great Tower

France is one of the largest countries in Europe. The **landscape** is mostly flat, but France does have some very high mountains called the Alps. The highest peak in Western Europe, Mont Blanc, is in the Alps. Mont Blanc is more than 15,000 feet (4,572 meters) tall. That's as tall as 12 Empire State Buildings stacked one on top of the other!

The land in France is **fertile**, so more than half of the country is used for farming. France grows more wheat than any other country in Europe.

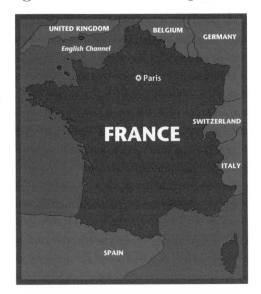

France's many rivers are all beautiful. The largest river is the Seine (sayn). It flows through the center of Paris, the country's **capital**. Paris is known all over the world for its palaces, fountains, museums, and gardens—and its great food!

Many beautiful castles stand along France's rivers.

One of the amazing wonders of France is the Eiffel Tower. This amazing **landmark** of iron and steel stands near the Seine River.

At first glance the Eiffel Tower looks like a toy tower made of thin wire, but it is very sturdy. Not even the strongest winds can challenge its strength. Do you know why this unusual-looking tower was built?

In 1889 there was a world's fair held in Paris. The French wanted to amaze people from other countries. Many famous people presented their ideas for building a tower. Gustave Eiffel had the winning idea. His plan was to build a tower with more than 2 million parts.

Putting the Eiffel Tower together took 300 workers and more than 2 years. It was the tallest building in the world until the Chrysler Building in the United States was built in 1930.

The Eiffel Tower stands at almost 1000 feet (305 meters) tall. Visitors can ride to the top in open-air elevators. Or they can climb up the spiral staircase, which has more than 1600 steps! They can even eat in a restaurant on the tower!

The Eiffel Tower lights up Paris at night.

When the Eiffel Tower was built, many people thought it was ugly. Others said it was unsafe. Today the tower is the glory of the Paris skyline. More than 5 million people visit it each year. The tower weighs several tons, but its pressure on the ground is the same as that of just one person sitting in a chair!

At night, lights on the Eiffel Tower shine across the city. It's no wonder that Paris has been nicknamed the City of Lights!

CHAPTER TWO
Guatemala's Giant Jaguar

Deep in Central America lies the country of Guatemala. Its landscape is full of mountains, forests, and volcanoes. Guatemala is the home of the highest mountain in Central America.

Guatemala has been struck by some wild hurricanes. Volcanoes and earthquakes have destroyed whole cities. Yet none of these disasters have destroyed the beauty of this colorful country.

Guatemala's rainy, warm weather and rich soil are home to many kinds of **exotic** flowers. Chicle (CHIHK uhl) trees grow in the rain forests. Chicle is used to make chewing gum.

Visitors to Guatemala can see macaws and other kinds of parrots flying through the forests. The national bird of Guatemala, the quetzal (keht SAHL), is one of the most beautiful birds in the world. Visitors should beware, though. Jaguars can be found in Guatemala, too.

The people of Guatemala work hard, but they also love to celebrate special days. The streets of the cities are often full of music and fun. Crowds of people dress in colorful costumes. Many celebrations in Guatemala have parades, fireworks, and masked dancers.

The tail feathers of a male quetzal are almost 3 feet (91 centimeters) long.

The Maya Indians are the native people of Central America and Guatemala. The ancient Maya created the first written language in the Americas. They made books of paper from tree bark. They also studied the moon and stars and invented a calendar.

Farming was very important to the ancient Maya. They believed the jaguar helped them with their crops. To honor the jaguar, they built a fantastic pyramid with a **temple** on top. The pyramid and its temple are called the Temple of the Giant Jaguar.

Many people are amazed that the Maya cut and moved huge stones to build the pyramid. They had no metal tools, and the wheel had not yet been invented. But these are not the only mysteries.

The Temple of the Giant Jaguar was built in Tikal. Although Tikal was a very important city for the ancient Maya, all its people left. No one really knows why the Maya left Tikal. For hundreds of years, the jungle of Guatemala grew over the beautiful temples and covered most of the city.

The Temple of the Giant Jaguar towers over Tikal, Guatemala.

The city remained hidden for a thousand years. Then a Spanish priest discovered it in 1695. More than 3000 buildings were uncovered. The Temple of the Giant Jaguar was the biggest and the best. Today the Temple of the Giant Jaguar is one of the most famous landmarks in Guatemala.

CHAPTER 3

Italy at an Angle

Italy is a country famous for its natural beauty and its works of art. On a map it looks like a boot ready to kick a football. The football is Sicily, the largest island in Italy. Sicily has Mount Etna, one of the largest active volcanoes in the world. The boot part of Italy is a **peninsula**. It is surrounded by three different seas.

Italy's landscape has sandy beaches, rolling hills, and two mountain ranges. The Alps tower across northern Italy. Another chain of mountains runs the length of the peninsula.

In Venice, people often travel by water.

Italy has several famous cities. In Venice the streets are actually waterways. People travel in **gondolas** instead of cars. Rome is the capital of Italy and the home of the Colosseum. Long ago, strong men fought in contests at the Colosseum. Celebrations and parades were held there, too.

In the city of Pisa stands a most unusual tower. The famous Leaning Tower of Pisa looks as if it's about to fall over at any moment. A trip to the top lets visitors see the Italian landscape at an angle. Do you know why this famous building leans?

The soft, sandy ground started to sink when the tower was being built. The tower was leaning even before it was finished. Every year the tower leans a tiny bit more. Although many people think the tower will tip over someday, it has been standing for 800 years! Writing on the tower tells us that it was started on August 9, 1173. It was finished about 200 years later.

The Leaning Tower of Pisa was built as a bell tower. It is 8 stories high. The top story contains the bells. Its columns are made of marble. Inside, a staircase with 294 steps winds its way from the bottom story to the top.

Would you dare to climb all the way up the Leaning Tower of Pisa? Galileo, a famous Italian scientist, climbed the tower's steps. He did some of his well-known science experiments at the top of the tower.

Even though it leans, Italians are very proud of the tower. Building experts from all over the world have offered ideas to straighten it. By 1990 the tower had been straightened about 1 inch ($2\frac{1}{2}$ centimeters).

CHAPTER 4

India Celebrates Beauty

On a map India looks like it is a large triangle pointing toward the Indian Ocean. India is a very large country with many long and wide rivers. Its landscape has forests, deserts, mountains, prairies, swamps, and green fields.

Parts of India have rain every day for half the year. Rice is grown in those areas. People also grow oranges, tangerines, grapefruit, and lemons.

India has many kinds of wild animals. Tigers, leopards, hyenas, elephants, rhinoceroses, and monkeys can be found on the land. Hippopotamuses and crocodiles are found in the rivers.

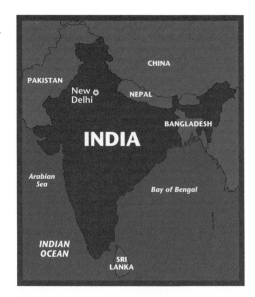

India's beautiful landscape includes part of the Himalaya Mountains. The word *Himalaya* means "house of snow." The Himalayas are the highest mountains in the world. They lie along the northern and eastern **borders** of India. The highest Himalayan mountain in India is 28,208 feet (8598 meters) high.

India's people have many interesting **customs**. Some women wear colorful saris (SAHR eez). A sari is a dress made of a single piece of cloth. The cloth is fastened at the shoulder and sometimes covers the head. Men wear turbans, long strips of cloth tied in a knot around the head.

The Himalayas—where the earth meets the sky

A famous landmark of white marble sits on the banks of an Indian river. The building is called the Taj Mahal. The name means "crown palace." But the Taj Mahal is not a palace. It is actually a tomb.

The ruler of India in the early 1600s was Shah Jahan. His wife Mumtaz Mahal died in 1629. Shah Jahan had the Taj Mahal built in her memory. It is a symbol of his love for his wife. More than 20,000 workers worked 22 years building the tomb. When Shah Jahan died, he was buried beside his wife in the Taj Mahal. Their bodies are buried under one of the rooms.

During the day, the walls of the Taj Mahal are so white that they sparkle in the sunlight. A huge dome crowns the top. At the corners of the Taj Mahal stand four small towers. They look like guards standing on the alert. Precious stones and paintings of flowers line the walls inside the tomb. Like the Himalayas, the Taj Mahal reminds us of the beauty of India.

The Taj Mahal

CHAPTER FIVE

In the Land of Hercules

Long ago the people of Greece made up stories to try to explain the world around them. These stories are called **myths**, and many of them have heroes. Have you ever heard of Hercules? He is a hero in many Greek myths.

Greece is well known for its myths. It is also famous for its ideas about freedom and justice. Greek art and ways of thinking have spread throughout the rest of the Western world. Ancient Greek ideas about government, the arts, math, and sports are important parts of life today.

Greece is a peninsula. Just as Italy looks like a boot, Greece looks like a hand. Greece also has more than 500 islands, so no spot in the country is far from the sea. Maybe this is why the Greeks have always been good at fishing and sailing.

Greece has many mountains. Most of the land is rocky. Even though the rocky land cannot be farmed, it gives the Greek landscape much of its beauty. The landscape also has white towns and villages, fields of grain, olive trees, and hills reaching out to the sea.

Greece is a country of rocky mountains and clear blue water.

Many beautiful temples once stood in Athens, the capital of Greece. The walls of those temples have crumbled, but many of the ancient marble columns remain.

The most famous temple in Greece is the Parthenon. Nearly 2500 years ago, a Greek ruler ordered that a temple be built on one of the highest spots in Athens. He wanted to build a beautiful temple to honor Athena. Athena was a goddess in Greek myths. She was greatly loved by the people of Athens. In fact, the city was named for her.

A famous **sculptor** placed a huge statue of Athena in the main hall. The arms of the statue were covered with ivory. The dress was made of pure gold. The statue's jewelry was made of real gems.

The Parthenon was made entirely of white marble. It had 8 columns at each entrance and 17 columns on each side. Above each entrance, the sculptor carved **festival** scenes and figures of brave warriors on horseback. Then these scenes were painted.

The Parthenon is an ancient wonder of the world. Over the centuries the temple has lost some of its beauty. The statue of Athena is no longer there. The figures above the entrances to the temple have lost their colors. But the Parthenon's sturdy columns still stand. The Parthenon is still admired by the whole world for its beauty.

The Parthenon in Athens, Greece

CHAPTER 6

A Great Wall

With more than a billion people, China has more people than any country in the world. It has nearly as many people as North America, South America, and Africa put together. China also covers a huge area of land. It is larger than the entire United States and almost as big as all of Europe.

China is famous for pandas. These animals do not live anywhere else in the world. China is also known as the birthplace of paper, the printing press, the clock, and fireworks. The people of ancient China invented all these things.

Beijing, the capital of China, is famous for its Forbidden City. It was named the Forbidden City because the early rulers did not allow anyone to enter it. But today anyone can enter and admire the wonderful palaces there. Many have unusual names such as the Palace of Eternal Spring, the Palace of Mountainous Beauty, and the Palace of Sweet Old Age.

Beijing's Forbidden City is almost 600 years old.

The Chinese people practice martial arts, such as karate and kung fu. More than 4000 years ago, they invented the game of soccer.

Long ago many countries built walls to keep enemies out. China has the longest wall of all.

China's Great Wall is often called the longest **monument** in the world.

More than 2000 years ago, the emperor Shi Huang ordered that the Great Wall be built. In those days armies traveled on foot. A wall was

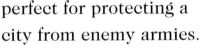

perfect for protecting a city from enemy armies.

The Great Wall of China was built by 300,000 soldiers and 2 million other workers. Earlier rulers had built walls of mud and stone. Shi Huang ordered these old walls to be repaired and joined with new ones. Shi Huang was the first ruler to think of and build a Great Wall.

The Great Wall of China stretches for thousands of miles across the country.

By 1400 much of the wall was falling apart. The ruler of China had the Great Wall rebuilt with bricks. This wall remains today. It is about 4000 miles (6400 kilometers) long and runs across mountains, valleys, plains, deserts, and rivers.

In many places the Great Wall is 16 feet (5 meters) thick. It is so wide that 5 horses can walk side-by-side on top of the wall.

The highest spots along the wall have the best view, so special watchtowers were built there. When enemies came near, the Chinese soldiers sent warnings to each other—smoke signals during the day or bonfires at night. The bigger the signal, the bigger the size of the enemy army. The message went from tower to tower until it reached the capital city.

No soldiers stand in the watchtowers of the Great Wall today. Instead, visitors stand and look out at the Chinese landscape. The Great Wall is an amazing landmark. Some people compare it to a dragon that stretches across China to guard the country.

The Great Wall of China has more than 10,000 watchtowers.

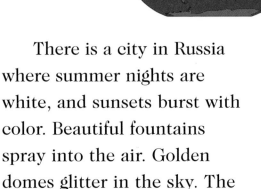

CHAPTER 7
Russia's Grand Palace

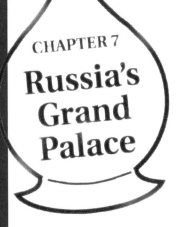

There is a city in Russia where summer nights are white, and sunsets burst with color. Beautiful fountains spray into the air. Golden domes glitter in the sky. The city is Saint Petersburg. It was founded by Peter the Great, a **czar**, or ruler, of Russia. The city was built near the Neva River.

Today Saint Petersburg is the second-largest city in Russia. It is a city of stone, just as Peter the Great wished it to be. It took 20 years to build the city. The czar used **architects** from all

over the world. That is why the buildings all have different styles.

Peter the Great conquered many countries and made the Russian Empire one of the largest nations in the world. Russia now spreads over two continents and has the largest land area of any country in the world.

Winters in Russia are very long and cold, especially in the parts closest to the North Pole. Some areas are so cold that no plants grow. Russia also has pine forests and prairies where grains grow, especially wheat.

Northern Russia is a land of snow and ice.

31

Many beautiful buildings lie along the waterways of Saint Petersburg.

Russia has some very long rivers. The Volga River is longer than the whole continent of Europe. Rivers like the Volga help unite the many people that speak more than 150 different languages. The country's customs, foods, arts, and monuments are as different as the people who live in Russia.

Among all the Russian landmarks, one stands out. It is the Grand Palace Petrodvorets (PIH truh dvuhr YEHTS). Peter the Great built this summer house facing the Baltic Sea in 1704. By 1723 he had turned the house into a palace with many incredible rooms. These rooms are decorated with beautiful things from all over the world—Turkish rugs, Chinese vases, French silks, and even tropical wood. Among the many treasures is a tiny model of the first roller coaster!

Today people come from every corner of the world to visit the Grand Palace. From the marble terrace visitors can view gardens with many marvelous fountains and waterfalls that reach out to the sea. The fountains and waterfalls have been working since 1721!

Peter the Great's Grand Palace

33

CHAPTER EIGHT

The Statues of Easter Island

Easter Island is an **isolated** place about 2300 miles (3700 kilometers) off the west coast of South America. Easter Island is a very strange place. It is famous for the giant stone statues scattered across the landscape. For centuries, only seabirds visited Easter Island. Now tourists come to see the fascinating statues.

How did this island come to be called Easter Island? It was discovered on Easter Day in 1722 by a Dutch explorer. He found native people who did not look like each other. Some were small and dark. Others were light with red hair. He also found, of course, the stone giants.

Easter Island has beaches of white sand.

Easter Island is one of many interesting islands off the west coast of South America. Here the sea has beautiful shades of blue—light blue, turquoise blue, and navy blue. Standing out among all the islands, of course, is Easter Island. Easter Island is very small, but it has beautiful fern forests and amazing views of the ocean. It is like a large outdoor museum. Easter Island belongs to the country of Chile.

Scientists still do not know where the people of this island came from. Were they from Asia or from South America? Wherever they came from, they had to be good sailors, because the nearest large area of land is more than 1000 miles (1610 kilometers) away.

More than 600 huge statues dot the island. The early islanders carved them hundreds of

Statues of Easter Island

years ago. Each statue was carved from a single piece of volcanic rock. The islanders set the statues on raised platforms. Large red stones were placed on some of the heads like hats.

The faces of all the statues look in the same direction—away from the sea. They have huge heads with long ears and no eyes. The heads sit on top of small bodies with no legs.

Most of the statues are 10 to 20 feet (3 to 6 meters) tall. The largest statue is about 40 feet (12 meters) high. That's nearly 7 times taller than an adult human!

How did the islanders manage to place the statues upright? Why do all the statues look in the same direction? What do they mean? These questions still have no answers. They are all mysteries yet to be solved!

Like Easter Island, our world is a huge museum. It is filled with landscapes and landmarks to learn about. You can visit the wonders of our world in person. Books can take you to them, too. Keep traveling!

GLOSSARY

architect a person who plans buildings

border a line that marks the edge of a country

capital the city where a country's government is

custom a group of people's way of acting or believing

czar a ruler of a country

exotic unusual; foreign

fertile rich in minerals; good for growing crops

festival a celebration

geography the land features of a region

gondola a long narrow boat rowed by a standing person and used on the canals in Venice, Italy

isolated away from other places

landmark a famous or well-known building or structure of historical value

landscape a view of natural scenery

monument a building, statue, or other object made to honor a person or event

myth a story that tells how something began

peninsula a portion of land surrounded by water on three sides

sculptor a person who carves things

temple a building to worship a god or gods in

INDEX